The Coconut Palm In Ceylon: Beginning, Rise, And Progress Of Its Cultivation

John Ferguson

In the interest of creating a more extensive selection of rare historical book reprints, we have chosen to reproduce this title even though it may possibly have occasional imperfections such as missing and blurred pages, missing text, poor pictures, markings, dark backgrounds and other reproduction issues beyond our control. Because this work is culturally important, we have made it available as a part of our commitment to protecting, preserving and promoting the world's literature. Thank you for your understanding.

THE COCONUT PALM IN CEYLON:
BEGINNING, RISE, AND PROGRESS OF ITS CULTIVATION.

No. 1.—From earliest Times to 1660 A.D. or the close of the Portuguese Occupation of the Maritime Provinces.

By the Hon. Mr. JOHN FERGUSON, C.M.G.

THE Coconut Palm has been the subject of several Papers included in the Journals of this Society. In the very first number, published in 1845, there is a Paper "On the Ravages of the Kuruminiya or Coconut Beetle," by J. Capper. The same beetle is referred to by Edgar Layard in the fourth issue of the Journal a few years after, in the course of a sketch on the Natural History of Ceylon. Again in Journal No. 5 the brothers J. G. and W. S. Taylor of Batticaloa contributed an interesting Paper "On the Manufacture of Sugar from the Juice or Sap of the Coconut Tree." In 1853 Mr. A. O. Brodie of the Civil Service contributed a statistical account of the Districts of Chilaw and Puttalam, in which reference is made to topes of coconuts along the sea coast, the total of the palms in the two districts altogether being then estimated at 950,000, covering about 12,000 acres. Then in 1882 we had brief references to the coconut palm from Ibn Batúta's account of his visit (in 1343) to the Maldives in the Paper translated for us by Mr. Albert Gray. And, finally, there is a reference to this palm in Johann Jacob Saar's Account of Ceylon in 1647–1657, translated for the Society by Mr. Freudenberg, Vice-President, in 1885. The traveller there speaks of "the many and beautiful trees called coconut trees" in the Island, and details some of the ways in which they are utilized; while he also mentions

that the numerous monkeys " do much damage to the trees."
[Mr. Geo. Wall in his Papers on an Introduction to a History of the Industries of Ceylon, vol. X., No. 37, 1888, makes no reference to the coconut palm.]

But nowhere throughout the Proceedings and Journals of this Society extending over a period of sixty years is there information afforded on a subject which, we might consider, should be of special interest to its members, namely, the first appearance and gradual spread, through cultivation, of the coconut palm in Ceylon. Unlike cinnamon, which is found growing wild as a tree in the jungles of the interior, the coconut palm (*Cocos* nucifera*, the Pol-gas or Pol-gaha of the Siṇhalese) is not indigenous to the Island. All that the late Dr. Thwaites, F.R.S., in his "Enumeratio Plantarum Zeylaniæ" says of this palm under "Habitat" is:

---

* Dr. Trimen mentions that "Cocos" is from the Portuguese name Coco or Coquo, given to the fruit from a fancied resemblance to a monkey's face. Marshall quotes Mr. Booth's Analytical Dictionary: "The three holes at the end of the shell give it the appearance of the head of a monkey." But he himself considers Coco is derived from the Greek word Kokos, a seed, nut, or shell. Baldæus, in his account of the idolatry of the East Indian Pagans, mentions how Ixora [Īsvara] turned the head of a man (beheaded by her) into a coco tree, "whence it is that the Indians say that the print of a man's face was fixed in the coconut." Early European writers up to the 10th century speak of it as "the nut of India," a term used by Robert Knox in the 17th century. Mudaliyár A. Mendis Guṇasēkara informs me that the Siṇhalese word "pol" is considered a pure original Siṇhalese word. He also writes: "Maharuk or máruk, another ancient Siṇhalese word for coconut, literally means the great or chief tree, and indicates that it must have been in the Island in great abundance from a very ancient date."

[The derivation of the name of the nut from Portuguese *coco*, "bugaloo," rests on the statement of Barros (Dec. III. III. vii.) and Garcia da Orta (*Col.* 16), whose books were both published in 1563. Barbosa (1516) says: "We [Portuguese] call these fruits *cocquos*." But the anonymous writer of the voyage of Vasco da Gama (1498-9) speaks of *ovquos* as if the name were the ordinary one, though the Portuguese had never seen the palm or fruit before this voyage (see Count Ficalho's remarks in his edition of Garcia da Orta's *Colloquios*, i. 247-50). See also *Hobson-Jobson*, s. v.

The word *pol* is derived by Professor W. Geiger (*Etym. des Singh.*) from Sanskrit *puṭa*, "funnel-shaped, hollow space;" Páli *puṭa, puṭi,* "vessel;" and he adds that in Sanskrit *puṭodaka* is coconut, lit. "having water in its hollow (fruit)."—D. W. F.]

"Commonly cultivated throughout the warmer parts of the Island." The late Dr. Trimen, F.R.S., in his "Handbook to the Flora of Ceylon," is more explicit, his statement being : "Universally cultivated throughout the low-country, especially near or on the sea coast; but not wild." A very experienced Ceylon coconut (as well as cinnamon, coffee, and tea) planter—Mr. W. B. Lamont, who first came to the Island in 1841, and still survives near Ratnapura—gives the following reasons, as the results of his observations in different districts of the Island, why the coconut cannot be regarded as indigenous :—

"We do not find in the coconut tree, as it appears in Ceylon, the characteristics of an indigenous plant ; we do not find it growing to maturity, and producing its seeds in the midst of the other natural growth ; but wherever Nature resumes her sway and maintains it for a few years on land in which this palm grows, we see it pine, cease to bear fruit, and ultimately die off ; the neighbourhood and agency of man seem necessary not only to its propagation and well-being, but to its existence. It is only found as a cultivated plant ; starved and neglected indeed it may be, but never totally abandoned to Nature for a long period of years."

Again, as Tennent so well puts it :—

"The presence of the coconut palm throughout Ceylon is always indicative of the vicinity of man, and at a distance from the shore it appears in those places only where it has been planted by his care. The Siŋhalese believe that the coconut will not flourish 'unless you walk under it and talk under it'; but its proximity to human habitations is possibly explained by the consideration that if exposed in the forests it would be liable, when young, to be forced down by the elephants, who delight in its delicate young leaves.

"In the deepest jungle the sight of a single coconut towering above the other foliage is, in Ceylon, a never-failing landmark to intimate to a traveller his approach to a village. The natives have a superstition that the coconut will not grow out of sound of the human voice, and would die if the village, where it had previously thriven, became deserted."—*Tennent, vol. I., p. 119, fifth edition.*

Then again Sir Samuel Baker, after eight years of wanderings in Ceylon jungles, remarks :—

"Groves of coconut trees towering over the thorny jungles often become monuments sacred to the memory of an exterminated village, and wild elephants generally overturn (ownerless) coconut palms, luxuriating in the succulent tops." *

De Candolle—I suppose, the greatest authority on the subject—places the original habitat of the coconut palm in the Eastern Archipelago, somewhere in the neighbourhood

---

* On the other hand, Simon Casie Chitty (in his "Ceylon Gazetteer," 1833) has no doubt about the coconut palm being indigenous. Here is how he introduces the subject :—

"Among the trees indigenous to the Island (if we except cinnamon, which furnishes the greatest item of its commerce) the claims of the coconut tree appear to predominate. Such is the benefit which this tree confers on the natives, that it is celebrated in song by the ancient bards; and one of them [whether Siṇhalese or Tamil is not mentioned] thus elegantly expresses the quality of its fruit in a Sanskrit stanza :—

> Usaggra uásé nacha pakshí rájá [1]
> Jalanta tárí nagato na méghá
> Subbrahma chárí nacha chandro máya
> Trínétr dhárí nacha Iswaránám. [2]
>
> It resides on high—yet it is not the king of the birds;
> It yields water—yet it is not the raining cloud;
> It is white—yet it is not the moon;
> It has three eyes—yet it is not Iswara.

[1] The Garuda, a bird sacred to Vishṇu, and consequently worshipped by his votaries. It is the Pondicheri eagle of Brisson, and its origin and history form the subject of one of the eighteen Puránas.

[2] Iswara is one of the mystical names of Síva, who is represented with three eyes."

Mudaliyár Guṇasékara reminds us that the coconut is mentioned in the great Indian epic *Mahábhárata*; and the Sanscrit *dákshiṇátya*—one of the names of the palm—literally means "native of the south." The "Materia Medica" of the Hindus compiled from Sanscrit medical works makes mention of various medicinal properties and uses of the coconut. The Mudaliyár adds that the name of the coconut tree in Tamil (*tennei*) seems to mean the southern tree, this tree having been brought, according to tradition, from Ceylon. So also says Dr. Caldwell in his grammar the Dravidian languages; but this is quite consistent with the view that the coconut originally came to Ceylon from the farther south-east.

of Sumatra and Java, and surmises that nuts floated thence both east and west—eastwards to the islands of the Pacific and the coast of Central America, and westward to Ceylon and India and the east coast of Africa. He considers that the introduction of the coconut into Ceylon, India, and China does not date back beyond 3,000 years; but that it floated by sea to the coasts of America and Africa at a more remote epoch. The native Siŋhalese tradition that locates the earliest specimen or grove of this palm in the neighbourhood of Weḷigama, on our southern coast, is in strict accordance with what might be expected under De Candolle's theory. [A glance at the map of Asia would seem to show how readily coconuts could float from Sumatra to Ceylon. After the eruption of the volcano Krakatao in Java, in August, 1883, the south-east shores of Ceylon were invaded by tidal waves carrying ashes and other *débris*.] The tradition is that a king of Ceylon was a leper, or afflicted with some skin disease, and that he (Kusta Rája) was cured by sea-bathing and the milk of the coconut, or the use of its expressed oil. The legend goes on to say that the king found no people where he found the coconut palm of his dream, as if to testify to its introduction through nuts carried across the sea from Sumatra and taking root on the sea coast near Weḷigama.*

---

* The affinity of a great majority of the genera (represented on our Ceylon south-west coast) is distinctly Malayan as opposed to Indian.—*Trimen*. Curiously enough to Trimen's remark " Coconut cultivated throughout the tropics, the origin is not known," Sir Joseph Hooker adds : " Indigenous according to Kunz in the Cocos and Andaman Islands." But Dr. Henry Marshall, Deputy Inspector-General of Army Hospitals, writing in 1836, says : " It is remarkable that the coconut tree has never been introduced into the *Andaman Islands*, although it is very extensively cultivated in the Nicobar Islands, which are within 30 leagues of the little Andamans." Evidence, I believe, has been afforded within historic times of the coconut taking root of itself after floating across the sea ; but a curious case of prematurely jumping to a conclusion occurred in 1890 to a distinguished botanist, who wrote to the London weekly, *Nature* :—

Self-Colonization of the Coconut Palm.

The question whether the coconut palm is capable of establishing itself on oceanic islands, or other shores for the matter of that, from seed cast

The fullest version I have seen of the "Traditional account of the original discovery of the coconut tree, by an ancient Siŋhalese Prince of the Interior of the Island of Ceylon" is

---

ashore, was long doubted ; and if the recent evidence collected by Professor Moseley, Mr. H. O. Forbes, and Dr. Guppy, together with the general distribution of the palm, be not sufficient to convince the most sceptical person on this point, there is now absolutely incontrovertible evidence that it is capable of doing so, even under apparently very unfavourable conditions. In the current volume of *Nature* (page 276) Capt. Wharton describes the newly-raised Falcon Island in the Pacific ; and in the last part of the Proceedings of the Royal Geographical Society Mr. J. J. Lister gives an account of the natural history of the island. From this interesting contribution to the sources of the insular floras we learn that he found two young coconut palms, not in a very flourishing condition, it is true ; but they were there, and had evidently obtained a footing unaided by man. There were also a grass, a leguminous plant, and a young candle-nut (Aleurites) on this new volcanic island—a very good start under the circumstances, and suggestive of what might happen in the course of centuries.—*W. Botting Hemsley* (*Nature, April 5, 1890*).

This was answered in the following issue :—With reference to Mr. Hemsley's note on this subject to *Nature* (page 587), I regret to have to inform him that the two young palms found on Falcon Island were placed there by a Tongan Chief of Namuka, who in 1887 had the curiosity to visit the newly-born island, and took some coconuts with him. This information I received from Commander Oldham, who had been much interested at finding these sprouting nuts at some 12 feet above sea-level and well in from the shore of the Island, but who found out the unexpected facts in time to save me from making a speculation somewhat similar to Mr. Hemsley's.—*W. J. L. Wharton* (*Nature, April 24, 1890*).

A writer in the *Journal of the Indian Archipelago* for 1850 observes that the tendency of the coco palm to bend above the sea, causing its fruit to drop into the water, appears to account for its extension to the numerous islands and atolls to which the nut is floated by the winds and tide. The little island of Pulo Merga off Sumatra, not a mile round and so low that the tide flows over it, is of a sandy soil and full of coconut trees, although at every spring tide the salt water goes clear over the island—so fond is the palm of the sea and salt.

"Essentially littoral," says Dr. Hartwig, in his *Tropical World*, "this noble palm requires an atmosphere damp with the spray and moisture of the sea to acquire its full stateliness and growth ; and, while along the bleak shores of the northern ocean the trees are generally bent landward by the rough sea breeze, and send forth no branches to face its violence, the coco, on the contrary, loves to bend over the rolling surf and to drop its fruits into the tidal wave. Wafted by the winds and currents over the sea, the nuts float along without losing their germinating power, like other seeds which migrate through the air ; and thus, during the

in the *Ceylon Miscellany* for July, 1842. A much more concise statement (which I give as a note) was sent to me some years ago by the late Mr. W. N. Rájapakse, Proctor of the Supreme Court.*

lapse of centuries, the coco palm has spread its wide domain from coast to coast throughout the whole extent of the tropical zone. It waves its graceful fronds over the emerald isles of the Pacific, fringes the West Indian shores, and from the Philippines to Madagascar crowns the atolls or girds the sea-border of the Indian Ocean. But nowhere is it met with in such abundance as on the coast of Ceylon, where for miles and miles one continuous grove of palms, pre-eminent for beauty, encircles the 'Eden of the Eastern Wave.' Multiplied by plantations and fostered with assiduous care, the total number in the Island cannot be less than twenty millions of full-grown trees [the estimate of 50 years ago.—J. F.]; and such is its luxuriance in those favoured districts, where it meets with a rare combination of every advantage essential to its growth—a sandy and pervious soil, a free and genial air, unobstructed solar heat, and abundance of water—that, when in full bearing, it will annually yield as much as a ton's weight of nuts—an example of fruitfulness almost unrivalled even in the torrid zone."

* THE TRADITION RESPECTING THE INTRODUCTION OF THE COCONUT INTO CEYLON.

(By the late Mr. W. N. Rájapakse, Proctor, Supreme Court.)

1. Kusta Rája (so called because he was afflicted with a cutaneous distemper) is the first person whose name is associated with coconut cultivation. He was a provincial king or prince in the midland parts of the Island. His disease having baffled the skill of his physicians, he was going about seeking a cure. On the beach of the sea coast somewhere near Weligama he found a coconut tree growing there and bearing fruit. The tree is supposed to have grown from a nut washed on shore from some foreign land. He drank the water of the nut either out of curiosity or by advice, and probably repeating the dose he got cured. This induced him to make a plantation of coconuts in the vicinity of Weligama. The result having proved beneficial to man, his image cut out of the solid rock was placed by the people of the place to perpetuate his memory.

2. Kusta Rája is believed to have lived after the conquest of the Island by Wijaya, and there are reasons to suppose that the coconut was known in Ceylon in the time of our first king.

3. The worship of certain gods, devil-dancing, and *bali* or invocation of the flowers were observed in Ceylon in the time of Wijaya and before that, and in all these three things the coconut plays an important part. In worship of gods the oil of the nut is used for lighting the lamps, and it is preferred to all other oils, except scented oils. In devil-dancing,

Curiously enough, the *Mahāwaṇsa* (the ancient Siṇhalese history of Ceylon) does not contain nearly so many references to the coconut as it does to the palmyra palm, probably

---

and *bali* a coconut is placed at the feet of the patient, and the devil-dancer concludes the ceremony by imploring that the ailments of the patient may descend to the coconut.

4. The invocation consists of the repetition of a number of verses which are herewith enclosed. This poem was composed by Totagammuwe Srí Ráhula, the Shakespeare of Ceylon, who by the way was a contemporary of the Bard of Avon, though they lived in different countries and were unknown to each other. In the commencement the poem sets out that the coconut was imported into Ceylon to be placed at the feet of Wijaya on the occasion of a *bali*, intended perhaps to avert the evils of his ingratitude to Kuvéṇi and murder of her people. According to this poem the home of the coconut was beyond seven seas. Then it goes on to describe the different kinds : the king-coconut, the scoert-husked* coconut, the diminutive coconut, and the *tembili* or the first-mentioned kind, being the one from which the other kinds sprang. Before this poem was composed in Siṇhalese it is believed that the same existed in Sanskrit, like most of the *mantras* or charms used in devil-dancing, but it was rendered into Siṇhalese and versified for facility of learning it by heart and to please the patient by its melody. This poem bears on it the impress of antiquity and is full of poetic genius and fire : no one now living can compose poetry like this, I think. This poem is repeated throughout Ceylon.

5. If this statement of importation of the coconut be true, this is a new and important fact, and Kusta Rája must at once be deprived of the credit of being the first finder of the nut and the honour be given to whom it is due. In this connection it is interesting to be reminded that the coconut tree flourishes best in that part of the Island where Wijaya reigned.

1. පළමු විජ නිරිඳු   ව
    පැමිණි විතදෙස හරිණ   ව
    සිරිපා තබන්තා   ව
    නැතුව සිටියසි තැඹිලි එමවි   ව

2. අසිරන් තැඹිලි ද   තා
    කොසි රට ඇද්ද ඇසුතා   තා
    සත්මුහුදෙන් එදෙසි   තා
    ගෙනා අසිරන් තැඹිලි මෙලෙසි   තා

---

* "*Scoert-husked* coconut" puzzled me somewhat ; but I am inclined to think "*scoert*" stands for the Dutch *zoet*, sweet. It is this description of coconut which I believe Mudaliyár Guṇasékera translates *Navase* (see page 9). *Navase*, I know, is a kind of coconut with a sweetish husk which, when tender, is eaten with great relish by the villagers.—*R. G. Anthonisz*.

because the latter, flourishing in a drier region, was better known at that time in North Ceylon and in India. Tennent finds an explanation in the fact that the *Mahâwaṇsa* was

3.	ගනිදු අවතාරෙ	ස්
	නාල්කෙස්රය විලසි	ස්
	විපත දුරලන මෙ	ස්
	එරස් තැඹිලිඳ උපත පවස	ස්
4.	එරස් පොල් ගෙනෙන	ව
	යස්නෙ කවුද ඇසුවි	ව
	අනඳමහතෙර සි	ව
	ගෙනැත් දුන්නයි එපොල් විගස	ව
5.	සත්බුහුදක් ඇත එකර එදෙසි	න
	ඉරුගල් බිසවගෙ කුසෙසි උපන්තැ	න
	ගනදෙවියො දුස් කිරුලිස දරමි	න
	සත් දින පසුවි පැලපත දකිමි	න
6.	යුදෙස් වැවුසු ගනදෙවියන්ගෙ කි	ස
	ගොසින් වැටුනි මහ හිමයක නිතිඉල	ස
	විගසින් සක්රජ බැඋවෙ දිව ඇ	ස
	එගොසිං වැවකටු තරකර සොඳලෙ	ස
7.	දිනෙස් දිනට වැඩෙමින් උසය	ස්නෙ
	රියස් පමන කැකුලසි අටග	ස්නෙ
	මුදුත ඉර අතු ගොබ නිල්ව	ස්නෙ
	ගොසින් වාත සුලඟට නදඳෙ	ස්නෙ
8.	සරියට තුමමස ගියතැන ඉසිරු	ති
	එලියට වන් මල් ඉති අනඹරල	ති
	පිරියට විමැසි බඹරෙනඳඳෙ	ති
	සරියට පොල් පස්වගයක් පලග	ති
9.	පලමුව රන්තැඹිලියනත් පොල්වෙ	ති
	දෙවනුව ගොන්තැඹිලියනත් පොල් වෙ	ති
	තුන්වෙනු නවිසිඳ බොඳිරිකැස් වෙ	ති
	සමසක් ගියතැන පොල්ගෙඩි මෝර	ති
10.	පොලවෙ මිසිකත ගසමුල වැසෙ	ති
	මහකෙලනාරජ කඳමැද වැසෙ	ති
	නාපති සුරපති කර බඩ වැසෙ	ති
	විස්නුඳ සක්රජ ගෙඩියෙ වැසෙ	ති
11.	තුස්තෙත් ගනදෙව් කිරුලිස ඇඳි	නා
	දුස්තෙත් මෙ පොල් ගනදෙව් විසි	නා
	පස්තිස් යාගය මතුරෙ දෙස	නා
	පොල්ගෙඩියට හෑම දෙසය බසි	නා
12.	පලමුව ඉසිවර වැවු උපති	ස්නෙ
	කැඳුව තරම ගනදෙව් තුමරු	ස්නෙ
	ඉසිවර දෙවියා නෙත් තුනඳු	ස්නෙ
	එරන්තැඹිලි තරලොවට උප	ස්නෙ

written by residents in the interior of the Island, while the coconut palm grew along the sea coast. One shrewd surmise why the *Mahāwaṉsa* has so little to say about the

---

13. ඉසිවර ලොගොසින් ගනිදු ඉසකඩාලා ගැසුතැ   සේ
    පුරඳුරු විත් එකිස අරගත ගැසිය තුස්ගවු පමණි , සේ
    එමසර සක් රජුගෙ ලැයිනේ එකිස රස් තැබිලියළු   සේ
    පැහැසර එනැඳු ලැයිනෙන් පැමිණි පිරිපත දුරුළ   සේ

The translation was made for me some years back, at the instance of Mr. H. C. P. Bell, C.C.S., by the late learned Chief Translator to Government, Mudaliyár B. Guṇasékera, and runs as follows :—

Translation.

1. In by-gone days a king-coconut could not be had when King Vijaya wanted one to put his noble feet upon (on the occasion of a ceremony intended) to avert a severe calamity.

2. On inquiry he was told that a king-coconut of golden colour might be had in a country on the other side of the Seven Oceans. He procured it in the following manner.

3. In order to remove the calamity it assumed the form of Ganésa (a Hindu god) typified by Nalikéra (a term for coconut in general). I am going to give an account of the origin of the golden *tembili* (king-coconut).

4. When a question arose as to who would go to fetch the *tembili*, the great Tera (Buddhist priest) Anada immediately brought and gave it.

5. At the end of seven days from the coronation of the wise Ganésa, born in the womb of Queen Irugal (who lived) in a country beyond the Seven Seas, the germ was seen.

6. Ganésa was defeated in a battle and his head fell in an extensive forest. Sakra, with his divine eyes, observed it in an instant and enclosed it with a strong fence.

7. It (the head metamorphosed into a coconut plant !) grows daily and attains height, with flowers of a cubit in length. Its young shoots become green and rustle before the wind.

8. At the end of full three months the flowers burst open with pedicles loaded (with tender fruit) at the tips. The bees alighting with joy make a noise on them. The tree bore five kinds of coconut.

9. The *first* was "ran-tembili" (king-coconut of golden tint), the *second* was "gon-tembili," the *third* "navisi," *fourth* "bodiri" (the *fifth*, not specified). After six months the fruits ripen.

10. The goddess of the Earth lives at the foot of the tree ; Mahakela, the snake-king, at the middle of the trunk ; the elephant-king and the god-king (Sakra) at the top ; while Vishnu and Sak-king live within the nut.

11. Ganésa, the three-eyed god, wearing a crown on his head, has given this coconut. By the efficacy of the incantations now used in

coconut, hazarded by the late Mr. H. Nevill of the Civil Service, is that the practice of toddy-drawing after a time, and its distillation into spirit, would prejudice the priestly historians against the palm and its cultivation.

The very earliest references to the coconut in the *Mahá-waṃsa* are more or less legendary, the first especially, when we are told in chapter XXV., page 98 :—

"During the battle between Duṭugęmuṇu and Elála (about 161 B.C.) Gotha (one of the former's warriors) is said to have seized a coconut tree and Mahasona (another warrior) a palmyra tree — with which they slaughtered the Damilas."

The next, from the same chapter, page 140, is quoted by Tennent as the very earliest mention of the coconut. It is simply mentioned as being known in Rohuṇa to the south, 161 B.C.; and again, the milk of the small red coconut is stated to have been used by Duṭugęmuṇu in preparing

---

connection with the 35 *yagas* (sacrifices or religious ceremonies) may every misfortune come down to this coconut.

12. In the first place, the eminent sage brought (it) into existence. The divine Prince Ganésa cut it up. The divine Íswara (Siva) gave it three eyes. Hence the appearance of golden king-coconut in the world.

13. Íswara went and broke the head of Ganésa, Sakra picked up this head and threw it up to a height of 3 *gaw* (12 miles). Then it became *ran-tembili* in Sakra's beautiful pleasure-garden : (hence) the present calamity has been removed.

[The usual nonsensical language of native charmers and kapurálas and kaṭṭaḍiyas (god-priests and demon-priests).—B. G.]

To another Siṇhalese gentleman still in our midst, we are indebted for the following : "The earliest mention of coconuts occurs in a story known as the 'Kuweni Hella.' It is stated there that Wijaya was afflicted with a dire skin disease and was roaming about in despair when he came across some fruits fallen under a tree which grew wild, which he ate, being quite unaware that it was wholesome, and discovered its wholesome properties, and that this fruit was the king-coconut. The date of this compilation and the author are unknown. One thing is certain, that when the compilation was made the tradition was prevalent in the Island, that at the date of the Wijayan invasion coconuts grew wild on the coast of Ceylon, and that neither the indigenous Yakka population nor the invading Aryans of Northern India knew the use of it."

cement for building the Ruwanweli Dágaba (*Mahâwaṇsa*, chapter XXX., p. 169).*

But the strange fact (remarks Tennent) is that notwithstanding these and other very early references nothing is said of the coconut as an article of food, nor is the palm given in the list of fruit trees to be planted, before 1153 A.D., Prakrama I. (*Mahâwaṇsa*, chapter LXXII.).

But before we come to this date we have the passage in chapter XLII., first brought to light by the late Mr. H. Nevill, C.C.S., which records how King Agrabodhi I. about 589 A.D. caused "a coconut plantation of three *yojanas* (about 36 English miles) in extent" to be formed, probably between Dondra and Weligama, and so it is surmised that his statue was cut out of the rock near the Weligama Viháré as a memorial of the king who introduced coconut planting into Ceylon.

This is doubtless the *very first* record of the formation of a *regular coconut plantation* in Ceylon; but that there must have been many palms growing before this time on the southern coast, and more especially around the port of Galle, we know from independent authority. Even Ælian, the Roman Historian, so far back as the middle or end of the 2nd century speaks of the sea coast of Ceylon as covered with palm trees (possibly referring to palmyras in the North and coconuts in the South). Chinese writers of the 5th century—when Galle was a chief port for the exchange of trade between East and West—mention "coconuts" and "arrack" (distilled

---

* "Philalethes" (Dr. Robt. Fellowes, M.A.) in his summary of Siṇhalese history has a curious statement, apparently from Valentyn, but not traceable in the *Mahâwaṇsa*. It runs : "Muta Singa Raja (the Mutasiva of the *Mahâwaṇsa*, who reigned 60 years) planted in the wilderness a great grove of coconut trees to which he gave the name of Mahamuna." In chapter XI. of the *Mahâwaṇsa* we are told the King Mutasiva formed the delightful royal garden Mahámégha (so called because of an unseasonably heavy fall of rain just as it was being laid out) which was provided in the utmost perfection with every requisite, and adorned with fruit- and flower-bearing trees of every description;" but no mention is made of coconut, nor indeed is any fruit specified at all.

from the coconut palm) as produced in Ceylon. Elsewhere in the same century the coconut is spoken of as the palm tree that bears "the great Indian nut;" and curiously enough Robert Knox, 1,200 years later, writes of the same palm as if it belonged to India rather than Ceylon.* Writing in 520 A.D., Sopater described Ceylon as surrounded by a multitude of exceedingly small islets (referring to the Maldives) " all containing fresh water and coconut palms."

Henry Marshall (Deputy Inspector-General of Army Hospitals in Ceylon about seventy years ago), who published a Monograph on the Coco Palm in 1834 (2nd edition, 1836), begins by stating: "The earliest notice of the coco tree which the author has seen is contained in an account of the travels of two Mohammedans in India and China in the 9th century." This reference seems to have been chiefly to arrack, and was about 810 A.D.

The fact is that a very backward part of Ceylon up to 1000 A.D. or later was the south-west coast, where the palm grew; the people seem to have been of the aborigines or Veddás, so primitive were their ways, and any trade was in the hands of the Moors, who up to the beginning of the 16th century controlled all commerce,† but these

---

* "Here are also of Indian Fruits, coker-nuts"—*Knox*, page 28 (edit. 1817); and that is all he has to say, although he gives a long account of the areca, talipot, jak, kitul, cinnamon, &c.

† This is what Tennent says: " During the middle ages, when Ceylon was the Tyre of Asia, these immigrant traders (the Moormen) became traders in all the products of the Island, and the brokers through whose hands they passed in exchange for the wares of foreign countries. At no period were they either manufacturers or producers in any department; their genius was purely commercial, and their attention exclusively devoted to buying and selling what had been previously produced by the industry and ingenuity of others. They were dealers in jewelry, connoisseurs in gems, and collectors of pearls; and whilst the contented and apathetic Siŋhalese in the villages and forests of the interior passed their lives in the cultivation of their rice lands, and sought no other excitement than the pomp and ceremonial of their temples, the busy and ambitious Mahometans of the coast built their warehouses at the ports, crowded the harbour with their shipping, and collected the wealth and luxuries of the Island, its precious stones, its dye-woods, its spices, and ivory to be forwarded to

same Mahommedan traders do not seem to care to mention the coconut or arrack, and for good reasons. The celebrated traveller Marco Polo, about 1300 A.D., speaks of the people in some parts of Ceylon as having for " their drink coconut toddy " or "wine drawn from trees."* This use of the palm is sufficient to explain why so little is made of it by the pious Buddhist writers of the *Mahâwaṇsa*, as also by Mahommedans, equally zealous in abstention from intoxicants.

To return now to the *Mahâwaṇsa*, we find that in chapter LXXIV. (page 214) the following passage occurs, giving the coconut a special position among the fruit-bearing trees planted by order of one of the greatest of Siṇhalese kings:—

" He (Prákrama Báhu, 1164–1197 A.D.) also adorned both sides of the road with fruit-bearing trees, as the king-coconut, plantain, areca, coconut, and such like, and with water jars filled with bunches of beautiful flowers, and with many kinds of banners and flags, and with lamps, censers, and such like."

Then of another great king, much given to travel and to make his ministers travel too in order to keep such roads

---

China and the Persian Gulf." Again: "The Siṇhalese mode of trading with the Chinese, Arabs, or Moormen long continued precisely the same as that adopted by the Veddas of the present day, namely by barter, the parties being concealed from each other, the one depositing the articles to be exchanged in a given place, and the others, if they agreed to the terms, receiving them unseen, and leaving behind what they give in return."

* Edrisi, the most renowned of the writers on Eastern Geography who wrote in the 12th century, in his account of Ceylon, mentions that the islanders cultivate rice, coconuts, and sugarcane; although the only exports he gives are precious stones, crystals, diamonds, and perfumes. A Chinese author so late as 1211 A.D., in speaking of the trade and products of Ceylon, only specifies "Cardamoms; cinnamon, coarse and fine; and mangrove." And even in 1611 the trading report is of cowries, cinnamon, pepper, gems, and elephants as obtainable in the Island. But may this indifference not be explained by the bulky nature of the nut, even when unhusked, and ignorance at the time as to any special value of the oil beyond its local use?

and bridges as then existed in repair—Prákrama Báhu II. (1240-1275 A.D.)—we find that he is said to have thought within himself, saying :—

"Great indeed his (Minister Dévapatirája's) piety, for once he prayed that he might become a Buddha, and planted a coconut, having earnestly prayed and resolved (that some sign should be shown him that his desire would be fulfilled), and lo, there opened up three buds from the three eyes thereof." And the king ordered his minister (among other things)—"At the Bhímatittha Viháré, where the King Nissaṅka planted an orchard, do thou likewise, in my name, lay out a large garden full of coconut and other fruit trees."

Then as the outcome of the king's thought it is recorded in the same chapter (14th verse) :—

"Thence this great minister proceeded to the port of Bhímatittha. And there he built a bridge, eighty-six cubits span, at the mouth of the Kalanadi* river ; one of about 100 yatthis† span at the village Kadalisena ;‡ one of 40 yatthis span over the Salaggama§ river ; and one of 50 cubits span over the Salapadapa∥ river. Thus did he build these and other bridges at divers places where it was difficult to cross over ; and likewise also he made numerous gardens and halls for preaching and the like, and did even give away much arms and hold feasts (in connection herewith).

"Afterwards this great minister of the king formed a large coconut garden, full of fruit and fine shade, and gave it the famous name Prákrama Báhu ; and it extended from the Bhímatittha Viháré (Bentoṭa) unto the ford of the Kalanadi (Kalu-gaṅga), a space of about one yójana in width.

---

* The Black river, Kalu-gaṅga.
† A yatthi is equal to seven cubits of two spans to the cube.
‡ Kehelsen, Kehel-lenáwa ?
§ Salgamu-gaṅga.
∥ Salruk.

"And when he had caused the great forest Mahálabujagaccha* to be cut down altogether and rooted up, he made a fine village thereon and planted a large grove of jak trees near it."

This shows that a coconut plantation was formed in the 13th century between Kalutara and Bentoṭa "one yójana" or 12 English miles "in width" (really in length) along the coast as it extended from the Bentoṭa Viháré to the ford on the Kalu-gaṇga. (The distance of the road between Bentoṭa and Kalutara in the present day is a little more than 11½ miles.)

The next mention is in the 90th chapter, which is as follows: "He also gave for the benefit of that Piriveṇa a village named Salaggama near the bank of the river Gimha (Gin-gaṇga), and in that delightful village of Titthagama (Toṭagamuwa) he formed a grove with 5,000 coconut trees." This was in the reign of Prákrama Báhu IV., who was surnamed Pandita Prákrama Báhu, whose seat of government was Kurunégala, and reigned in 1295 A.D.

There are two further references to the coconut in the *Maháwaṇsa*; but as these are so recent as the 18th century, they will come in more properly into the second division of my Paper, which is to embrace Dutch and British times.

The slow progress made in the cultivation of a palm so pre-eminently beneficial, in purely Siṇhalese times, is no doubt accounted for by the seat of monarchy and authority being (for the most part) so far in the interior, and population congregated chiefly in the north-central and central districts, while the south-west coast was at that time comparatively sparsely occupied.† During several centuries, even after the important plantations formed by order of their kings, the Siṇhalese people, we may suppose, did not

---

* Mádelgasvanaya.

† King Prákrama Báhu sent in the 12th century to reduce the South of Ceylon.

do much to extend the cultivation of the coco palm beyond what might be needed for the supply of their own families. Indeed they had no object or special inducement to do so; for the produce could not be carried very far inland (in the absence of roads) with the means of transport at their command, and there is no evidence to show that the nuts, oil, or arrack were exported much before the end of the 15th century. Still by this time we may take it for granted that not only the people on the south-west coast from Kalutara round to Dondra Head, but also many of the villagers farther north and farther inland had begun to realize the value of the coco palm. To Mudaliyár Simon de Silva, the learned Chief Translator to Government, I am indebted for references which bear out the view that coconut gardens had been formed by this time in the Western Province even up to the banks of the Kelani-gaṇga. I append in a note the references given by the learned Mudaliyár to classical works other than the *Maháwaṇsa*.* A Chinese writer who describes Ceylon about the year 1413 A.D. writes of "the coconut which they have in abundance supplying them with oil, wine, sugar, and food."† It must have been about this time that the enterprising Moormen who commanded all the foreign commerce began to turn the coconut to account. At first undoubtedly, being Mohammedans, they would have nothing to do with arrack as an intoxicating spirit, and not much was at the time known of the value of the oil, while

---

* 1. In the 71st and 76th verses of the Girá Sandésa, a poem written in the 15th century, reference is made to coconut gardens in the Pánaduré and Kalutara Districts.

2. In the 107th verse of the Paravi Sandésa, written about the same time, mention is made of a coconut garden beyond Balapiṭiya.

3. In Kovul Sandeṣa references are made to coconut gardens in the Southern Province.

4. In the 42nd verse of the Selalihini Sandésa of Toṭagamuwa, who flourished in the reign of Prákrama Báhu VI. (1415 to 1467 A.D.), reference is made to coconut trees growing on the bank of the Kelani-gaṇga.

† "Ceylon Literary Register," vol. IV., 1889-1890, page 118.

the nuts were far too bulky a freight, in proportion to value, to be carried like cinnamom, gems, or silk all the way to Arabia or up the Red Sea for transport overland to Europe. But evidently a market nearer home, in the North-West of India was discovered; for, although the South of India may have had palms enough of its own* to make Robert Knox (160 years later) speak of the coconut as an Indian rather than Ceylon fruit; yet further up, beyond Bombay and along the Cambayan coast, the coconut produce of Ceylon found a ready market. This I gather from the very first experience of the Portuguese at Colombo recorded in Gaspar Correa's history of the doings of his countrymen in India and Ceylon during the first half of the 16th century.† For instance, we are told of Dom Lourenço de Almeida's arrival in 1506—that "as he entered the harbour there were many vessels (Moor) which were loading cinnamon and small elephants, in which there is great traffic to all parts, chiefly Cambaya, and in this port they were also loading green coconuts and dry ones, from which is extracted oil, and much *arequa*, all of which is much prized in Cambaya; also masts, yards, and planks, Ceylon having a great supply of good wood." Then later on we read that the Sinhalese king (then at Kótté) sent the Portuguese Commander "a present of provisions for the whole fleet, consisting of abundance of fowls and figs (really plantains) and coconuts, which are all eaten with the shell on, and sweet oranges and lemons (limes)." And on Lopo Soares' departure in 1518, as a farewell gift, the king sent him "six rings of sapphires (worth 1,000 cruzados) and six small elephants (a fathom in height, easily shipped), with great abundance of eatables for the fleet, and especially so many coconuts that they piled

---

* That there were many coconut palms in Malabar when the Portuguese came to India we know from Varthema (1510) and Barbosa (1516), both of whom call the coconut *tenga* (Malayalam). See *Hobson-Jobson*, s.v. "Coco." —D. W. F.

† "Ceylon Literary Register," vol. III., 1889, page 133.

on the shore those that each inclined to load, and even then there were many over."*

The next reference we need quote is from the record of his experiences by the first Englishman who visited Ceylon. This was Ralph Fitch, who touched at Colombo in March, 1589, on his way from Bengal to Cochin, and who reports in the account of his travels : "This Ceylon is a brave land, very fruitful and fair; but by reason of continual war with the king thereof, all things are very dear. The provision of victuals for the Portuguese cometh out of Bengal every year." He speaks of the people as " black and little," and adds : " Their houses are very little, made of

---

* In " The Thousand and One Nights " or " Arabian Nights' Entertainment " (Lane's translation), written about 1475-1515 A.D., there are some amusing references to coconuts, no doubt gained from the experience of Mohammedan travellers in previous centuries. One occurs in the " Fourth Voyage " of Es Sindebad of the Sea, where he and companions got cast away among "a magian people " whose king was a ghoul, eating human flesh ; in addition to bringing strange food to fatten and stupefy them, they gave them " coconut oil " to drink, and also anointed their bodies with the oil, and all perished save Es Sindebad, who loathing, could not eat this food, and who got so emaciated as not to be worth the eating. Secondly, in the "Fifth Voyage," after his experience of "The Old Man of the Sea," on getting to the City of Apes, he was befriended by a man who gave him a bag to fill with pebbles and to go forth with a party, all similarly laden, to a wide valley having lofty trees which no one could climb, and also many apes which at the sight of the strangers ran up the trees, evidently coconut palms. For, on the men pelting the apes with the stones, the apes responded by plucking off the nuts and flinging them at the men, and in this way the latter collected a great quantity of coconuts ; and Es Sindebad did this for many days until he was able to sell a large quantity of nuts, " the price of which became a large sum in my possession." (To do this, the price must have been very different from that recorded for the Maldives 100 years later of 400 coconuts per larin, or equivalent of 8d. sterling.) This country from the context must have been the Malay Peninsula or Sumatra ; for, in returning to the Persian Gulf it is told they passed "by an island in which are cinnamon and pepper"—evidently Ceylon. And in the next or " Sixth Voyage," Es Sindebad, after an extraordinary fashion, came to " Sarandeeb " (the Arabic name for Ceylon), which he describes as to situation and area very fairly, and mentions much about its minerals and gems and lofty mountains and trees with spices, but not a single reference to coconut or any palm all the time he was there ; while, finally, the king sent him away with rich gifts (gems, &c.) to his own king, Kaleefah Haroun Er-Rashud.

the branches of the palmer or coco tree, and covered with the leaves of the same tree."

In view of the export trade in coconuts which the Portuguese discovered immediately on their arrival, in view also of the abundance of coconuts gathered no doubt from gardens in the Kóṭṭé and adjacent districts along the Kelani-gaṇga, nay probably from the neighbourhood of Colombo itself— while we know that the coast from Kalutara to Galle and on to Dondra Head was covered with the palm 400 years ago, as it is to-day—it is most astonishing that there is little or no mention of the coconut by the otherwise full and careful Portuguese writer Ribeiro, whose manuscript was presented to the King of Portugal in 1685. The areca (betel-nut) and talipot palms are freely mentioned; but the coconut scarcely at all. This would seem to show that the Portuguese never had much export trade in coconut produce;* that they esteemed it as of less importance than cinnamon bark, and the arecanut —both, of course, much more valuable at the time, in proportion to bulk, a matter for consideration in days when the biggest of their ships (small brigs and barques) would be deemed unequal even to a coasting trade in the present day. In the account of the arrival of the Dutch Admiral J. van Spilbergen off the south-east coast of Ceylon in 1602 it is mentioned that as they approached a bay they "found a great grove of coquos trees;"† and the French traveller Pyrard (1601-1605) gives a very full description of the coconut palm and its different products,‡ while he also reports having seen as many as 100 ships loaded with coconuts at the Maldives

---

* On the other hand, Barros, describing Ceylon (III., II., i.), says:— "It has great palm groves, which is the best inheritance of those parts; because, besides the fruit thereof being the common food, these palm trees are profitable for divers uses; of which food, called coco, there is here great loading for many parts." In III., III., vii., describing the Maldives, he treats at length of the coco and its uses. See also Linschoten, chap. 56 (partly taken from G. da Orta).—D. W. F. [Doubtless the shipments were for Indian and other Asiatic ports and not for Europe.]

† *Query*, Arugam Bay, see "Ceylon Literary Register," vol. VI., p. 316.

‡ "Ceylon Literary Register," vol. V., 1890-1891, p. 300.

(doubtless for Cambay and Persian ports); while 400 nuts were in these islands sold for a larin, a coin of about 8d. sterling or 50 cents of our rupee in value. (The Maldives have maintained a continuous export trade in coconuts—as their staple product—for, probably, 500 to 600 years at least. Percival records how early in the past century a ship from the Maldive Islands touched at Galle, which was entirely built, rigged, provisioned, and laden with the produce of the coconut palm.) Although such a Portuguese authority as Ribeiro took so little notice of the coco palm, we know from other contemporary writers that its cultivation was, by the beginning of the 17th century, attended to round many villages in the interior as well as on the coast. An interesting reference to this period is found in the diary of a Jesuit priest (Father Manoel Barradas) who travelled in 1613 with other priests as far inland as Seven Kóralés.* They were welcomed at several towns and villages, notably at Mattégama,† "capital of the Seven Corlas" (then an important town, "10 leagues from the coast," apparently situated about two miles from Giriulla between the Mahá-oya and Deyahandula) with decorations along the roadsides " of tender leaves of palms, hanging at one place and another cocos and bunches for those of our company to help themselves to them at their will," and so at some other villages on their way back to Madampé and Chilaw; but it must be noted that there is no mention of the palm growing at Madampé, Kalpitiya (Calpentyn), or Mannár at that time. It is of further interest to quote two passages from this Jesuit writer referring, first to coconut palms at Colombo in 1613, and secondly to palms generally in the Island :—

"As the Portuguese in the time of the kings of Ceilaõ possessed nothing outside the walls, on account of sieges being frequent, the same city served them as a palm-grove,

---

* See "Monthly Literary Register," vol. IV., 1896, page 129 *et seq.*

† Mattegama, in 1613 the then capital of Seven Kóralés and " a large town well laid out in streets," is now a poor little village, the change being possibly due to its malarious situation.

there not being a palm therein that had not been planted, even on the hill,* above the stones, as is even now seen; and the goodness of the soil and its coolness allows of all this. So that even now, after their being cut down (and they are going on every day cutting down many palm trees), the least that is visible is the city. This makes it a little sombre and melancholy, although inside it is becoming beautified with many and good dwelling-houses which look like palaces; and outside with many country-houses which have been and are being built with splendid houses and large enclosures; and they are already getting near to the river Calane, which is close upon a league."

Again: "There are in Ceilaõ all the varieties of palm trees that are distributed over the other parts of India, to wit, the White Trefolins,† the Cajurins,‡ Nipeira§ or Date-palms, but these wild ones; because though they yield fruit it is not fit for food. There are the Talapates, which bear a leaf so large, and united after the manner of the bat's wing, that of one alone is made an umbrella which can shelter three or four persons together from the sun and the rain. There are lastly the cultivated ones, which bear such large cocos that they are two and a half spans in circumference, particularly in Mateigama. Among the cultivated ones there is one variety in Ceilaõ which is not found in any other place; nor have I heard it spoken of until now. In our Castle of Columbo there is a palm tree whose bark, leaves, new and old, fruit in little lanhas‖ and afterwards cocos, always have a yellow colour, like that of gold;¶ and it may well be that

---

* St. Sebastian.—D. W. F.

† Kitul?—D. W. F.

‡ Areca ?—D. W. F.

§ See *Hobson-Jobson*, s. v. "Nipa." The *Nipa fruticans*, not the Date-palm, as the writer seems to imply.—D. W. F.

‖ Vieyra's Port. Dict. has "Lanha, s. f. (in Ethiopia), the fruit of the cocoa tree when it is tender and green." I do not know what the origin of the word is; but *cf*. Siṅh. lá, unripe, young, immature. From Tannilan-káy = unripe fruit.—D. W. F.

¶ The "King-coconut" is, of course, referred to.—D. W. F.

this is the branch of which the poet speaks: *Aureus et simili frondescit virga metallo.* I say this, because Virgil says of it, that it was the offering of Proserpina: *Hoc sibi pulchra suum ferri Proserpina munus instituit.* And of these palm trees, which many call royal from the beauty of the colour, but of which the Father Nicolao Paludano, of our Company, who travels about those parts, writes that with more reason they might be called *Luceférinas*, since the fruit is used by the heathen Chingalàs only for offering to the devil."

There is also a reference by this Jesuit priest to "Canals"—forty years before the arrival of the Dutch—which is worth quoting, though of no bearing on our immediate subject:—

"Near Columbo the Fathers embarked on a canal* by which they entered into the river Calene, and going down the river they proceeded into another canal as narrow as shady, so that the oars, although they were very short, could scarcely fulfil their office, and for a good distance the trees which intertwined their branches served them as a protection from the sun, until they came out into some level cultivated fields over which it was pleasant to the sight to gaze. By this they went as far as Negumbo, which is six Chingalà leagues. This canal was artificially made by the king when he was at war with the Portuguese; because the principal internal trade of the Island being by the river Calene, and its mouth being near Columbo, our people easily stopped it by sea; wherefore he diverted it by means of this canal, which is of no little convenience."†

This shows that canal communication between Colombo and Negombo was established by a Kandyan king (probably Don Juan Dharmapala, 1542–1584) long before the time of the Dutch, who usually get the credit of all our canal systems in Ceylon.

---

* St. John's Canal, probably.—D. W. F.

† The Muturájawila is doubtless the canal referred to. I do not know who was the king who constructed it.—D. W. F.

There is not much more to learn respecting coconut cultivation in the time of the Portuguese; and yet there is one reference dating from 1644-1649—seven to nine years before their final expulsion by the Dutch—which goes to show that if not valued by the historian or foreign merchant, the supreme importance of the palm as a food producer was duly recognized by the Portuguese occupants of the Island. We quote from Johann von der Behr's account of his experiences in Ceylon from 1644 to 1649* (he was a Cadet in the Dutch Service, and was attached to an invading army). It is where he describes the landing at Negombo and an island in front of it "on which stand more than 3,000 cocos or kochers trees," each tree bearing ten, twenty, or thirty small and large nuts, and later on he adds that from the branches, &c., of the palms, houses were made to accommodate 600 of the troops. The palm was for all uses, and he adds that "the Portuguese esteem the tree very highly, and say that if one shot a bullet through a tree and struck the heart (in consequence of which it would dry up) it was as if he had put a man to death."

Baldæus in his account of Ceylon, printed in 1672, should be able to show how the south-west and especially the north of Ceylon stood for palms at the time the Dutch arrived. He gives a very particular description of the different divisions, parishes, and churches in the Jaffna peninsula and islands; often refers to gardens with "Indian fruits" and "delicious vineyards," but seldom mentions the coconut. Of Mannár island, he only tells us it abounds in fish, so that here, as at Negombo, is a great industry in drying and sending large quantities to other parts. He refers to the fertility of the Mántota district in rice crops, and to the great mischief done by elephants which used to cross the river (lagoon) into Jaffna to feed upon the fruits of the palm trees, knocking these trees down. Recurring to the Jaffna churches, we are told of those at Changane, Paneteripo, and

---

* "Ceylon Literary Register," vol. VI., 1891-1892, page 82.

Batticotta as having behind "an orchard of cocoe and Portuguese fig trees, besides potatoes, bananaes," &c. Patchiarapalle was much infested with elephants, "by reason of the vast quantity of wild palm-trees* that grow here and afford food to the poorer sort of inhabitants, though the elephants threw down some hundreds every year, being very greedy after the fruit when it comes to maturity." This could scarcely be the coconut—evidently the palmyra. But in chapter XLVII., in referring generally to the people of Jaffna and the climate, Baldæus makes a statement which shows that to some extent at least the people cultivated coconuts. He mentions the eight months of dry weather when perhaps rain only falls three times, "which is the reason that they are obliged even to water the coco trees till they are six years old," and he afterwards refers generally to "Cocoes" in Ceylon. As regards the neighbourhood of the capital, here is a curious paragraph from Baldæus, referring to the beginning of the siege of Colombo : "The following day a certain Portuguese prisoner was brought into the camp ; he was sent from *Milagre*, and had lived fourteen days upon grass and herbs in the woods."† This would seem to show there were no coconuts in the woods near Milagraya, and indeed we know Governor Van Imhoff in the next century had jungle felled along the route from Colombo to Kalutara in order, under the rules of *rajakáriya*, to have coconuts planted by the villagers.

We can now sum up the position of the coconut palm in Ceylon about the middle of the 17th century, when the Portuguese occupation of the Maritime Provinces came to an end. In the first place we may venture to say that the cultivation was almost entirely confined to the south and west of the Island. There is little evidence of the coconut palm growing along the eastern coast, at any rate above Arugam Bay

---

* This is one of the translator's errors. The original has *palmeer* = palmyra.—D. W. F.

† See also chap. XXIV., under 19th October.

(Pottuvil) or Batticaloa; and there cannot have been many gardens of palms in the north. Robert Knox on his escape in 1679 gives an account of the products of the "Malabar" country through which he had passed to the north-west coast, and of which he had learned by observation and report. He says: "The commodities of this countrey are elephants, hony, butter, milk, wax, cows, wild cattel: of the three last great abundance. As for corn, it is more scarce than in the Chingulays countrey; neither have they any cotton. But they come up into Neure Caulava yearly with great droves of cattel, and lade both corn and cotton."*

From an account of the Jaffna peninsula in the Dutch times, when there were 150 villages (many more than in the time of the Portuguese), we learn these were all in the north of the peninsula; for in the south forests prevailed, full of elephants and other wild beasts; and so numerous and bold were the elephants that two of them waded across a lagoon near Jaffna and appeared in the streets of the town about the year 1660. We gather from this (and Baldæus) that the coco palms then cultivated were confined to certain villages in the north of the peninsula and a few in the islands. The palmyra was probably much more common. We take it, further, that up to this time the coconut had not been planted (unless a few here and there) at Maṇṇár, Kalpiṭiya, Puttalam, or Chilaw—indeed very few north of Negombo. Probably the Mahá-oya may be taken as the northern limit on the western coast; although farther inland the coconut palm was found around villages north of that river, in the Seven Kóralés, and generally near all villages throughout what is now known as the Western Province. At the same time, we cannot suppose—seeing what afterwards happened in the time of Van Imhoff—that there was much cultivation between Colombo and Kalutara. There were certainly some gardens near Colombo, more particularly in the direction of Kóṭṭé and the Kelani river as far inland as Sítawaka,

---

* Page 356, Robert Knox's "Historical Relation." edit. 1817.

but the great continuous extent of planting of which we are quite sure was from the Kalu-ganga, southward to Bentota, and from thence to Galle and on to Weligama, Matara, and on to Dondra Head. At the same time it is unlikely that this belt extended far inland, save where village topes or gardens broke the continuity of the jungle or chena land. The map which has been prepared through the courtesy of the Surveyor-General and of Mr. Templeton of his staff, and to which we now call your attention, indicates by different colourings the successive stages in the advance of coconut planting in Ceylon, so far as we are able to judge, from the information and authorities laid before you. We begin with a small patch of dark green colour with bars round Weligama, indicative of the spot where the earliest nut or nuts floated ashore from Sumatra, took root in the sand and gave Ceylon its first coconut palm, perhaps 3,000 years ago. There must have been a good deal of planting of the nuts in the neighbourhood and at intervals in the country towards Galle long before King Agrabodhi, according to the *Maháwaṇsa* in 589 A.D., gave the order to form a plantation from Weligama to Dondra. For, as already mentioned, the Roman writer Ælian about the middle of the 2nd century of the Christian era, or say 160 A.D., mentions on the authority of travellers that the coast about Galle was covered with waving coco palms, and further he records the notable fact that the palm trees grew *in regular quincunxes as planted by skilful hands in a well-ordered garden.* So we give in a second colouring (light green) a sweep of country that must have shown palms to voyagers up to 500 A.D. Then comes the historical planting of King Agrabodhi, 589 A.D., coloured brown by itself, and equally distinguished is the plantation ordered by King Prákrama Báhu II. along the twelve miles of country between the Kaluganga and Bentota, between 1240 and 1275 A.D., the colouring being light red. Before this time, however, there was planting (about 1100 A.D.) between Ambalangoda and Bentota, for which we have put in a dark red colouring. About the same period, or a little later, there were also certain roadside plantings of fruit trees (including the coco palm) by orders of King Prákrama Báhu the Great; but it is impossible to say with what success, especially as regards palms. Undoubtedly such kingly attention to this most useful of tree food-producers must have acquainted the people throughout many villages and districts with its value, and accordingly from the 13th century on to the middle of the 17th, when our observation closes for the present, the Siŋhalese throughout the low-country of the south-west, between Dondra Head and the Mahá-oya river, and in villages perhaps ten, twenty, or even thirty miles inland, as in Three and Seven Kóralés, became more and more alive to the value of a palm which so variously ministered to their comfort, entering into every part of their life as food, drink, light, fuel, household utensils, and building materials. We have accordingly added a sixth distinct colouring in sienna, for villages north of the Kalu-gaŋga in the Western Province, near Kóṭṭé, Colombo, along the Kelani-gaŋga, indicating gardens planted up to 1450 A.D.; and finally the seventh colouring (neutral tint) covers planting done between the middle of the 15th and 17th centuries (up to 1660 A.D.), north of the Kelani-gaŋga, about Negombo, in Seven and Three Kóralés, in a few gardens in the north of the Jaffna peninsula, and at Tangalla, Pottuvil, and Batticaloa. The wars which raged almost continuously for 150 years between the Siŋhalese monarch and the Portuguese must have sadly interfered with agricultural progress of any kind; and there was not the same strong inducement of a keen foreign demand which prevailed in the case of cinnamon and arecanuts, to induce a large export trade in coconut products. This trade indeed did not attract much attention till towards the end of the Dutch[*] and beginning of the British rule,

---

[*] I learn from Mr. Anthonisz, Government Archivist, that in the Instructions left for his successor by Governor Ryklof van Goens, in 1675, no reference is made to any trade in, or revenue from, coconuts, oil, coir, or arrack; although full mention is made of arecanuts, pepper, rice, elephants,

notwithstanding the enterprise of the Moormen traders as shippers of nuts to Cambay and Persia so early as the 14th to 15th centuries. At the beginning of last century the estimate was that there were 10 millions* of coconut palms in Ceylon. One hundred and fifty years earlier a safe estimate would in our opinion be about 8 to 8½ millions; for, we do not think there was much extension of cultivation by the people in the latter end of the 17th and 18th centuries, for reasons which will be given in our second Paper covering the Dutch and British periods to date. As centuries rolled by, it must be remembered there was always work for the people

---

and especially cinnamon. Twenty years later, by the year 1695, however, the Dutch rulers had discovered some value in coconuts as a source of revenue; and Jaffna cultivators were specially exempted from the coconut tax, because they supplied the leaves of the palm to feed the elephants belonging to the Government. But all this, with other interesting extracts Mr. Anthonisz can give from Dutch archives, belongs rather to the second part of my Paper.—Since writing the foregoing I have come across an Order in Council of the Dutch Executive in Ceylon, dated May, 1669 (translated by the late R. Van Cuylenburg, Esq., in a Paper for this Society's Journal, 1874, part I., page 69), which runs as follows:—" May, 1669.—The Council finding that the coconut plantation at Soute Tangh yields a revenue of not more than 1,260 rix-dollars per *annum*, against an outlay of 620 rds. per *mensem*, resolve on renting it out to the Burgher Louis Trumble (see Valentyn, *Ceylon*, 245) at 900 rds. per annum from the 21st June next to the end of February, 1671." The Government Archivist, Mr. Anthonisz, tells me that "Soute Tangh" must be a sort of hybrid equivalent (half Dutch, half Portuguese) for "Tanque Salgado," situated at Mutwal. Mr. Anthonisz writes: "*Tanque Salgado* is Portuguese for salt pond. The name is now applied to a pretty large tract of land in the northern suburbs of Colombo, below Fisher's Hill. It is evident the Portuguese either found such a pond, or made one, in the spot after their arrival here. But all traces of a pond have, I believe, now disappeared. In the oldest Dutch records the name is applied to a hamlet with a large population. I find it mentioned in a 17th century school thombu with other hamlets in the neighbourhood, such as *Horta Padre* (Priest's Garden), *Horta Juan Swaris* (Juan Swaris' Garden), *Goenwyck* (Goen's Retreat), *Horta Cadirane*" (Garden of Cadirane), &c. All the names are Portuguese except Goenswyck, which is called after the Dutch Governor Rycklof van Goens."

* Bertolacci in 1815.—Our estimate at the present time (1906) for all Ceylon is that there must be about 60 millions of coco palms growing, of all ages and conditions.

in replanting the area already occupied; for, although the coco palm is exceptionally long-lived, no one has ventured to put its productive bearing age at more than 100 years.

Discussion.

9. His Excellency the Governor invited remarks on the Paper.

Mr. C. M. Fernando referred to the archæology of the coconut. He would distinguish between the coconut of commerce and the special variety known as "the King coconut," a rarer and more precious variety, which was used for medicinal purposes. It was probably "the King coconut" that had attracted Kusta Rája's attention and cured him of his skin disease. The coconut was probably very much older in Ceylon. There was a Ceylon before Vijayo, just as there was a Rome before Romulus, and Generals before Agamemnon, and the coconut palm was probably much older than Kustá Raja. He said the Mahabárata and the Rámáyana mentioned the coconut palm, and the latter referred to its existence in Ceylon.

Mr. Ferguson pointed out that his argument was not at all based on the legend of the Kusta Rája; but that, according to the great authority of De Candolle, the dispersion of coconuts from Sumatra probably took place about 3,000 years ago.

Mr. Harward instanced the frequent way in which legends were created to account for misunderstood facts, and thought that Kusta Rája and the legend with him was probably of similar origin. He quite agreed with Mr. Fernando that there was a civilized Ceylon before Vijayo's time; and considering how much Ceylon was visited by traders from the North-West and Far East in very early times, he did not think the floating theory was necessary to account for the coconut being transferred and planted here.

His Excellency the Governor said that, before moving the vote of thanks, he felt it incumbent upon him as an archæologist to say a few words on the question raised by Mr. Fernando and Mr. Harward, and, after humourously referring to the very old legend of Ixora turning the head of a man into a coconut, as related in a note to the learned Paper before them, His Excellency proceeded:—Ladies and gentlemen, there is a very pleasant duty which devolves upon me, that of proposing to you a most hearty vote of thanks to our friend Mr. Ferguson for the treat that he has given us this evening. It is not often that the Society has such a treat as a Presidential Address, so teeming with most instructive matter, and at the same time a Paper by the same gentleman, so learned and full of interest as the Paper to which we have just listened.

In his Presidential Address Mr. Ferguson alludes to Polonnaruwa and the work that is being done there. Undoubtedly an immense amount of excellent work is being done at Polonnaruwa under the supervision of Mr. H. C. P. Bell. The excavations of the ruins have been suspended for a short time for the express purpose of enabling the Archæological Commissioner to make up his notes and bring his literary work up to the present time. It was impossible for him to continue the compilations of his work and at the same time carry on excavations, considering how extremely close personal supervision must be maintained by the archæologist over the work of excavation.

I was at Polonnaruwa not long ago, and while looking for one of the ruins, we lost ourselves in the woods. We wandered about for four hours and traversed several miles, and during the whole of that time we never took our feet off bricks which formed part of the buildings of the ancient city. That city must have extended over many miles, for, wherever we went, wherever we turned, we always found bricks, evidence that the place had been built over in the years gone by.

Mr. Ferguson has mentioned the zoological collection here. Well, ladies and gentlemen, there is a great difference between the very interesting collection in question and a really well-equipped zoological garden. But, in order to establish a zoological garden, one has to enter upon a very large expenditure. The matter was fully gone into last year and the year before. We found that the expenditure would be very great; and there were strong objections from many people against a large zoological garden being established in the vicinity. On the whole, I came to the conclusion that the present collection had better be left to the tender care of Dr. Willey to extend in due course, rather than to take his pets and place them in a zoological garden, where they might perhaps not be cared for and looked after as well as they are at the Museum.

There is one matter which struck me when Mr. Ferguson referred to the various directions in which Ceylon is advancing at the present moment. I was reminded of an interesting fact, a fact which is very complimentary to the Colony and its reputation for progress. To-day I had a letter from the Government of a Southern Colony. The letter informs me that they had come to the conclusion to help education there by giving two important scholarships on the results of their annual examinations; and having considered what was best to be done with those scholarships, they came to the conclusion that the soundest education for the boys would be to send them to the Technical College in Ceylon, and they asked me to give them information regarding the work of the Technical College, the fees, &c. The fact that such a decision has been arrived at by the Government of a Southern Colony is, I think, a very great compliment to this Island; and also, to a certain extent, an answer to some of the objections which people make from time to time against the work of the Ceylon Technical College.

Now, ladies and gentlemen, I have no doubt whatever that you will respond with acclamation to the proposal I make, to accord a hearty vote of thanks to the President, the Hon. Mr. Ferguson, for the admirable Address he has given us, for the interesting Paper on the Coconut with which he followed the Address, and for the pleasure with which we have listened to Mr. Ferguson.

VOTE OF THANKS TO THE PATRON.

10. The Hon. Mr. S. C. OBEYESEKERE proposed a vote of thanks to their Patron, His Excellency the Governor, for the encouragement which his presence had given them. His Excellency had had an arduous day—a journey from Veligama, a busy meeting of the Legislative Council, and the business of the Colony—and it was a proof of his extreme interest in the Society that he was able to be there in spite of all.

Mr. FERNANDO seconded.

The PRESIDENT heartily supported the vote. In the Society's past records the name of Sir Arthur Gordon ranked foremost among Governors for the interest he took in the Society; yet, short as Sir H. A. Blake's term had so far been, he had already eclipsed the previous record by the warm personal interest His Excellency took in the Society, and his very frequent presence at their Meetings.

The vote was carried with applause.

Printed by Libri Plureos GmbH in Hamburg,
Germany